AMERICAN INDIAN NEEDLEPOINT DESIGNS

for Pillows, Belts, Handbags & Other Projects

ROSLYN EPSTEIN

DOVER PUBLICATIONS, INC.
NEW YORK

To Miss Linda Ormesson, design consultant of the Embroiderers' Guild, whose guidance, inspiration and knowledge made my task considerably easier.

Published in Canada by General Publishing Company, Ltd., 30 Lesmill Road, Don Mills, Toronto, Ontario.
Published in the United Kingdom by Constable and Company, Ltd., 10 Orange Street, London WC 2.

American Indian Needlepoint Designs for Pillows, Belts, Handbags and Other Projects is a new work, first published by Dover Publications, Inc., in 1973.

International Standard Book Number: 0-486-22973-4
Library of Congress Catalog Card Number: 73-82422

Manufactured in the United States of America
Dover Publications, Inc.
180 Varick Street
New York, N. Y. 10014

INTRODUCTION

Needlepoint, an old embroidery form once called the art of queens, has never enjoyed more popularity than it does today. It is no longer the boring job of working a dark-colored background around a Victorian rose. Today's needlepoint worker wants all kinds of imaginative new designs to translate into needlepoint. The designs in this book are all adapted from authentic American Indian motifs.

It is a good idea to work out a detailed color scheme for the design before beginning a project. You will find tracing paper very convenient for this purpose. The illustrations on the covers of this book are executed in authentic Indian colors.

After you have worked out a color scheme the design may be transferred to the canvas. Since the designs are planned for working on a #10 needlepoint canvas— each square in the grid representing one stitch to be taken on the canvas—the design may be worked directly onto the canvas by counting off on it the same number of warp and woof squares shown in the diagram. You may prefer to outline your design on the canvas itself. Since needlepoint canvas is almost transparent, you can lay it over the designs in the book and trace the pattern directly onto the canvas. If you decide to paint your design onto the canvas, use either a non-soluble ink, acrylic paint thinned appropriately with water so as not to clog the holes in the canvas, or oil paint mixed with benzine or turpentine. Designs placed on the canvas can be colored in as an aid to the worker. Always make sure that your medium is waterproof. Felt tipped pens are very handy both for outlining or coloring in the design on the canvas, but check the labels carefully because not all felt markers are waterproof. Allow all paint to dry thoroughly before beginning any project.

There are two distinct types of needlepoint canvas, single-mesh and double-mesh. Double-mesh is woven with two horizontal and two vertical threads forming each mesh whereas single-mesh is woven with one vertical and one horizontal thread forming each mesh. Double-mesh is a very stable canvas on which the threads will stay securely in place as you work. Single-mesh canvas, which is more widely used, is a little easier on the eyes because the spaces are slightly larger.

A tapestry needle with a rounded, blunt tip and an elongated eye is used for needlepoint. The most commonly used needle for a #10 canvas is the #18 needle. The needle should clear the hole in the canvas without spreading the threads. Special yarns which have good twist and are sufficiently heavy to cover the canvas are used for needlepoint.

Although there are over a hundred different needlepoint stitches, the one that is universally considered to be "the" needlepoint stitch is the *Tent Stitch,* an even, neat stitch that always slants upward from left to right across the canvas. The stitches fit very neatly next to their neighbors and form a hard finish with the distinctive look that belongs to needlepoint. The three most familiar variations of Tent Stitch are: Plain Half-Cross Stitch, Continental Stitch and Basket Weave or Diagonal Stitch. The choice of stitch has a great deal to do with the durability of the finished project.

v

Plain Half-Cross Stitch, while it does not cover the canvas as well as the other two variations, provides the most economical use of yarn. It uses about one yard of yarn for a square inch of canvas. The stitch works up quickly, but it has a tendency to pull out of shape, a disadvantage that can be corrected in blocking. This stitch should only be used for pictures, wall hangings and areas that will receive little wear. It must be worked on a double-mesh canvas.

Continental Stitch, since it covers the front and back of the canvas, requires more wool than the Plain Half-Cross Stitch (it uses about 1¼ yards of yarn to cover a square inch of fabric). The stitch works up with more thickness on the back than on the front. As a result the piece is more attractive with better wearing ability. This is an ideal stitch for tote bags, belts, headbands, upholstery and rugs since the padding on the reverse saves wear on the needlepoint. The Continental Stitch also pulls the canvas out of shape, but this is easily corrected by blocking.

The Basket Weave or Diagonal Stitch makes an article that is very well padded and will wear well. It uses the same amount of wool as the Continental Stitch and does not pull the canvas out of shape. Since the stitch is actually woven into the canvas, it reinforces the back. This stitch is especially suited for needlepoint projects that will receive a great deal of wear, such as chair seats and rugs. Its disadvantage is that it lacks manueverability and is hard to do in areas where there are small shapes or intricate designs.

Plain Half-Cross Stitch: Always work Half-Cross Stitch from left to right, then turn

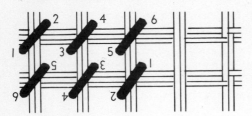

the canvas around and work the return row, still stitching from left to right. Bring the needle to the front of the canvas at a point that will be the bottom of the first stitch. The needle is in a vertical position when making the stitch. Keep the stitches loose for minimum distortion and good coverage.

Continental Stitch: Start this design at the upper right-hand corner and work from

right to left. The needle is slanted and always brought out a mesh ahead. The resulting stitch is actually a Half-Cross Stitch on top and a slanting stitch on the back. When the row is finished, turn the canvas around and work the return row, still stitching from right to left.

Basket Weave or Diagonal Stitch: Start the Basket Weave in the top right-hand corner

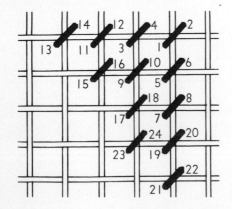

(left-handed workers should begin at the lower left). Work the rows diagonally, first going down the canvas from left to right and then up the canvas from right to left. The rows must be alternated properly or a faint ridge will show where the pattern has been interrupted. Always stop working in the middle of a row rather than the end so that you will know in what direction you are working.

When starting a project, allow at least a 2" margin of plain canvas around the needlepoint. Bind all the raw edges of the canvas with masking tape, double-fold bias tape or even adhesive tape. There are no set rules on where to begin a design. Generally it is easier to begin close to the center and work outward toward the edges of the canvas, working the backgrounds or borders last. To avoid fraying the yarn, work with strands not longer than 18".

When you have finished your needlepoint, it should be blocked. No matter how straight you have kept your work, blocking will give it a professional look.

Any hard, flat surface that you do not mind marring with nail holes and one that will not be warped by wet needlepoint can serve as a blocking board. A large piece of plywood, an old drawing board or an old-fashioned doily blocker are ideal.

Moisten a Turkish towel in cold water and roll the needlepoint in the towel. Leaving the needlepoint in the towel overnight will insure that both the canvas and the yarn are thoroughly and evenly dampened. Do not saturate the needlepoint! Never hold the needlepoint under the faucet as this much water is not necessary.

Mark the desired outline on the blocking board, making sure that the corners are straight. Lay the needlepoint on the blocking board, and tack the canvas with thumb-tacks about ½" to ¾" apart. It will probably take a good deal of pulling and tugging to get the needlepoint straight, but do not be afraid of this stress. Leave the canvas on the blocking board until thoroughly dry. Never put an iron on your needlepoint. You cannot successfully block with a steam iron because the needlepoint must dry in the straightened position. You may also have needlepoint blocked professionally. If you have a pillow made, a picture framed, or a chair seat mounted, the craftsman may include the blocking in his price.

Your local needlepoint shop or department where you buy your materials will be happy to help you with any problems.

AMERICAN INDIAN NEEDLEPOINT DESIGNS

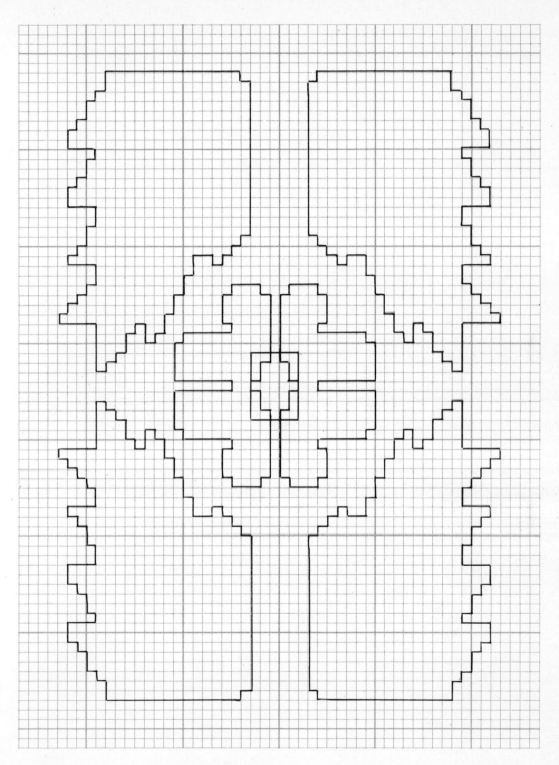

Design from Menomini (Algonquin) beadwork. Suitable as a repeat for tote bag or purse.

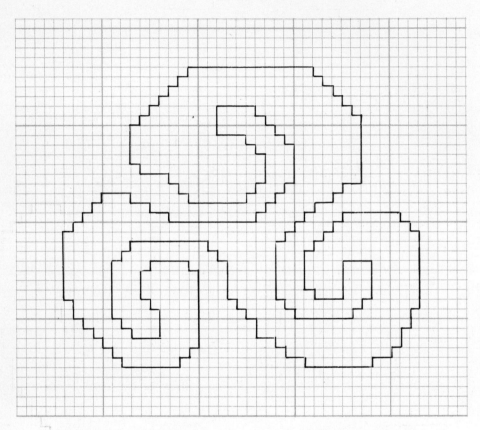

Motif from a Pre-Columbian Mexican flat stamp from Apatzingan
using curvilinear spirals. Suitable for pocket, small picture,
trivet or coaster.

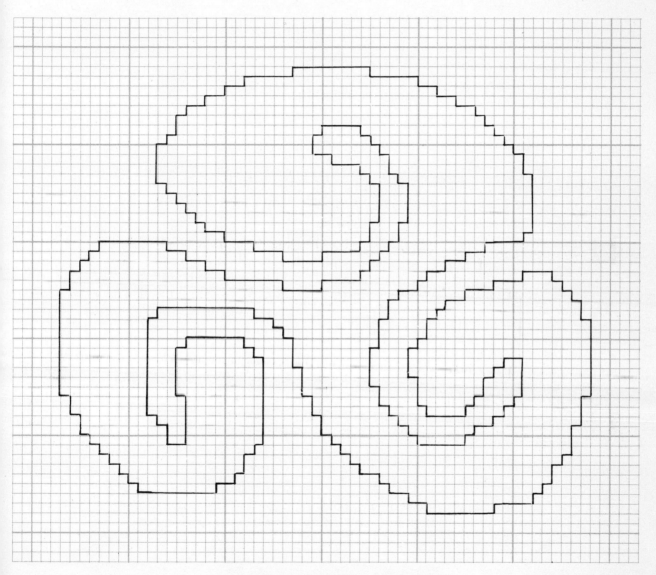

Enlarged version of motif on opposite page.

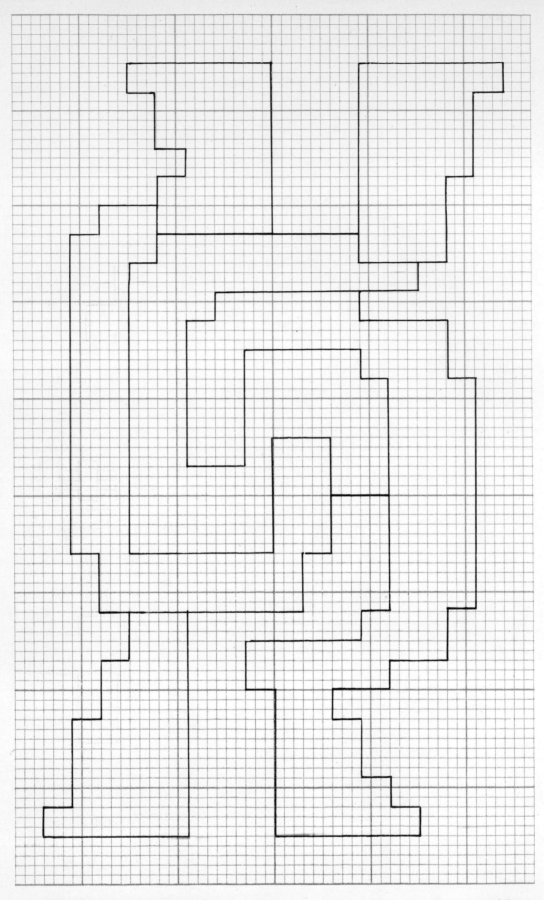

Adaptation of a Pre-Columbian flat stamp from Mexico City using the stepped-fret (Xicalcoliuhqui) pattern. Suitable for book cover or tote bag.

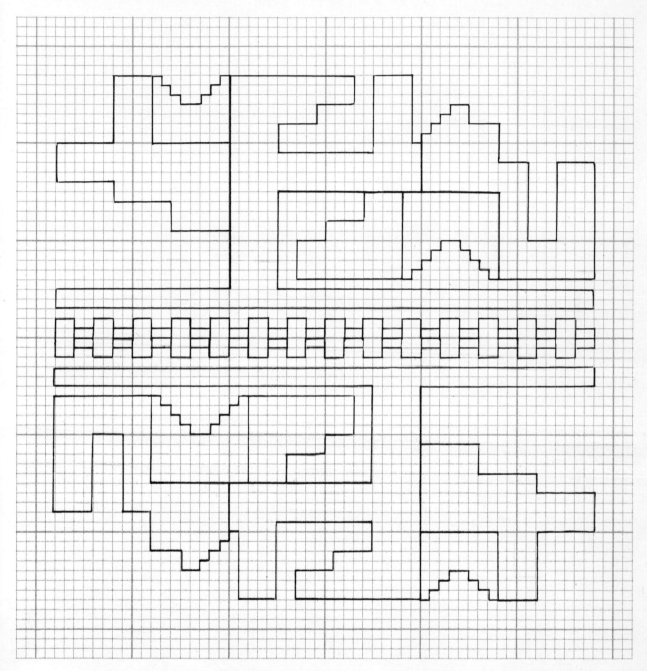

Motif from a Zuñi jar. Suitable for picture or, with an added border, as a small pillow.

Choctaw design. Suitable for picture, pillow or wall hanging.

6

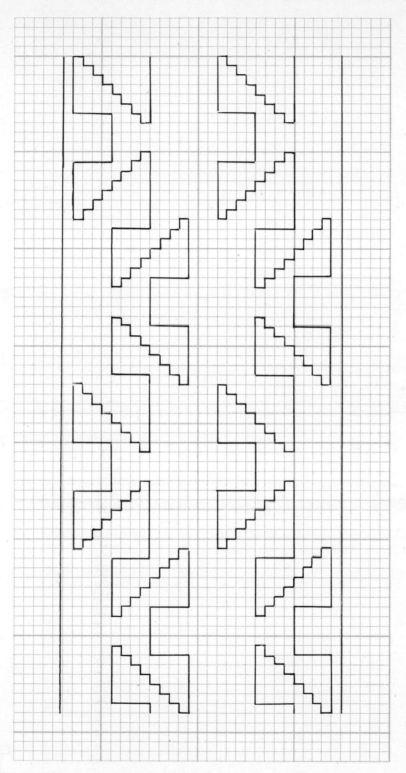

Yurok motif. Suitable for headband, belt or border design.

Motif from a British Guianan basket design. Suitable as a repeat pattern for rug, tote bag or pillow.

Columbian Mexican flat stamp from Vera Cruz showing deer (Mazatl). Suitable wall hanging, pillow or picture.

Choctaw design. Suitable as a repeat for rug or reverse repeat for pillow or tote bag.

(Left) Menomini (Algonquin) design. *(Right)* Choctaw design. Suitable for belt, head-band, mirror frame or border design.

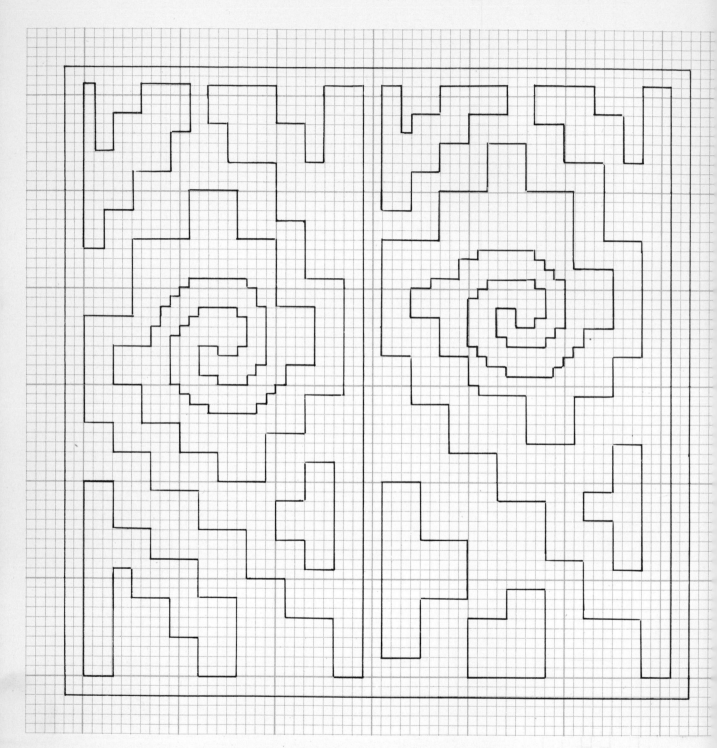

(*Above and opposite above*) Pre-Columbian cylindrical-stamp design found in Mexico City. Originally used on gourds, this stepped-fret (Xicalcoliuhqui) motif is here combined with the spiral. Above suitable for tote bag, pillow or picture. Opposite above suitable for pocket, patch, small picture or small pillow.

(*Right*) Variation on preceding Pre-Columbian design. Suitable as a border for m frame or tote bag, or as a repeat.

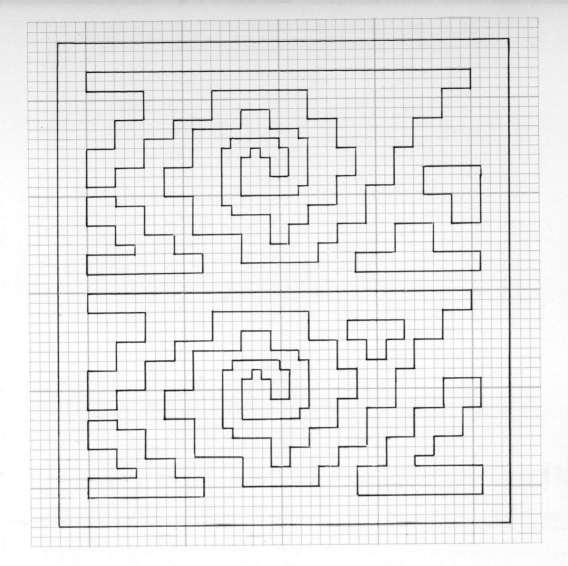

13

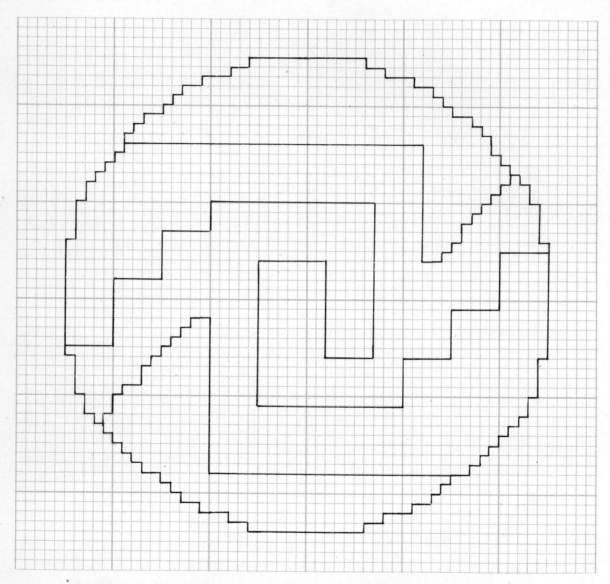

Adaptation of a Pre-Columbian Mexican flat-stamp design using stepped-fret (Xical-coliuhqui) pattern from Puebla. Suitable for pocket, patch, coaster, small picture or pillow.

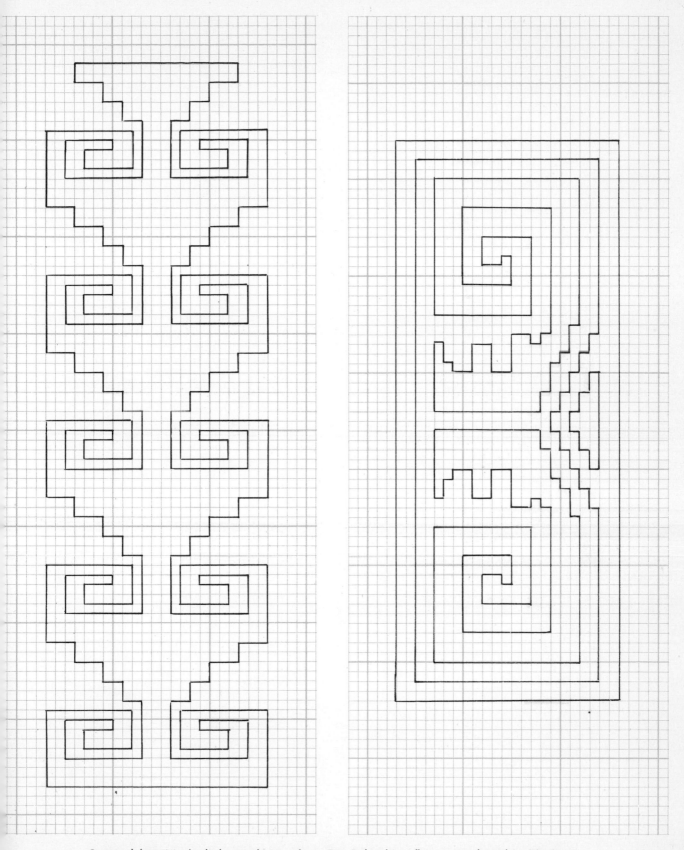

Stepped-fret (Xicalcoliuhqui) designs from Pre-Columbian flat stamps found·in Mexico City *(left)* and Guerrero *(right)*. Suitable for belt or headband, or as a border design on a book cover or tote bag.

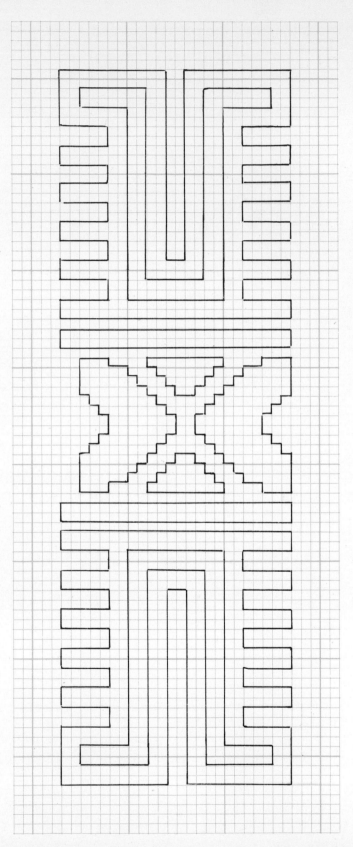

Pre-Columbian flat-stamp design from Mexico City. Suitable for belt or headband, or as a border design on a mirror or book cover.

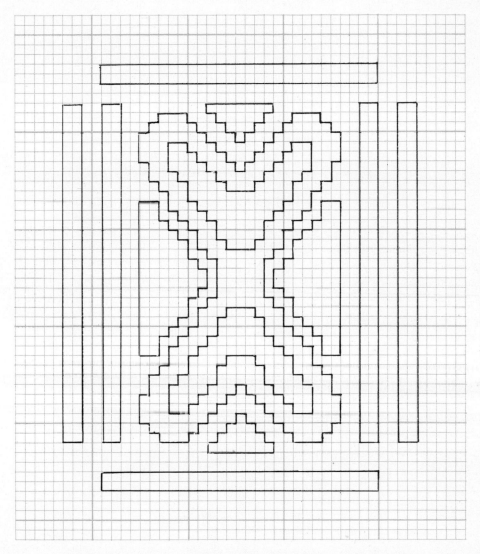

Motif from design on opposite page. Suitable for pocket, patch, small picture or as a repeat pattern.

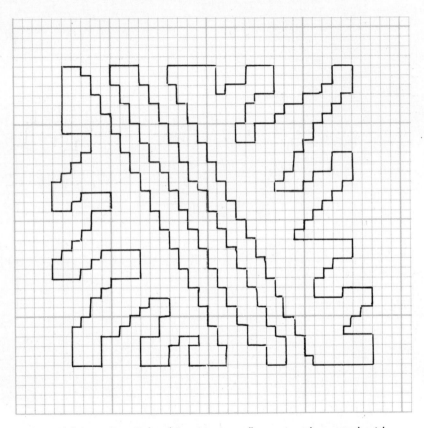

Motif from a Pre-Columbian Mexican flat stamp decorated with curvilinear spirals and angles. Suitable for pocket, patch, small picture or as a repeat pattern.

Another motif from the same Pre-Columbian Mexican flat stamp that appears on opposite page. Suitable for picture, pillow or tote bag.

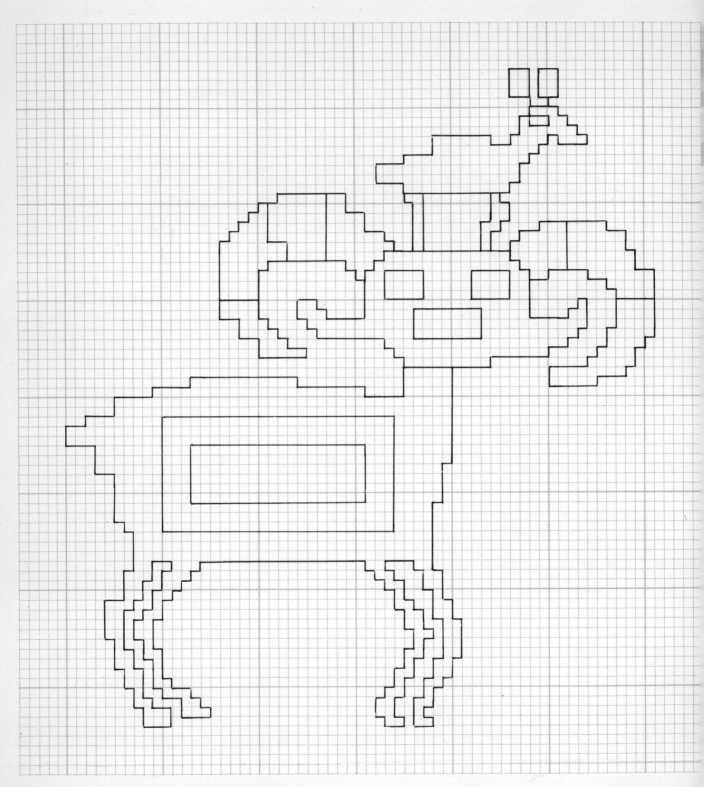

Black-and-white pottery design painted inside a bowl from the Mimbres Valley, New Mexico. Suitable for pillow or picture.

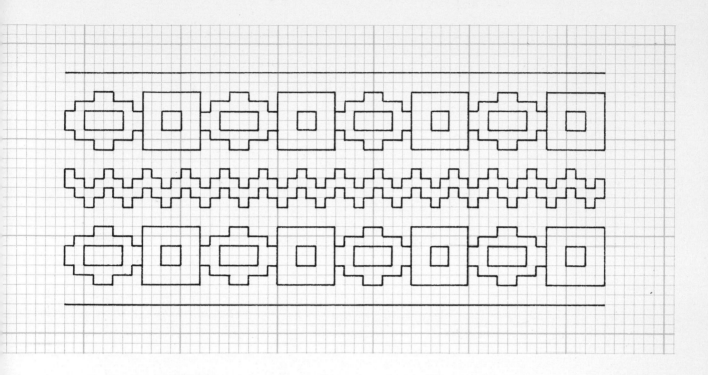

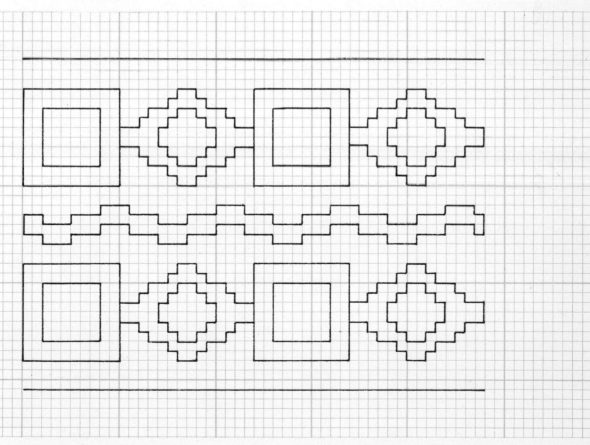

Variations on a Menomini (Algonquin) design. Suitable for belt, headband, luggage straps or change purse (with zipper across top); or as a repeat pattern on a pillow or as a border design.

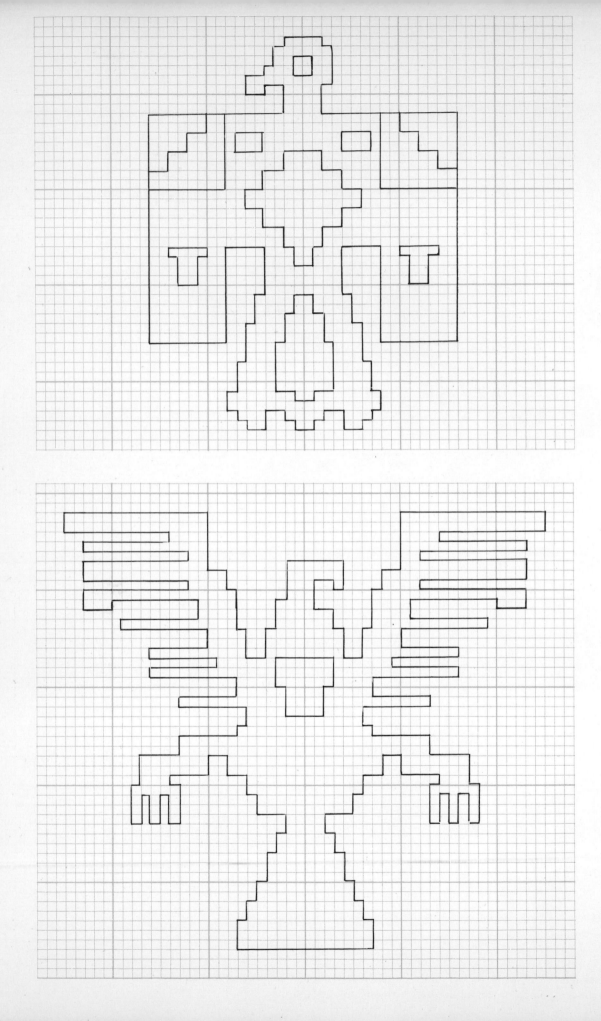

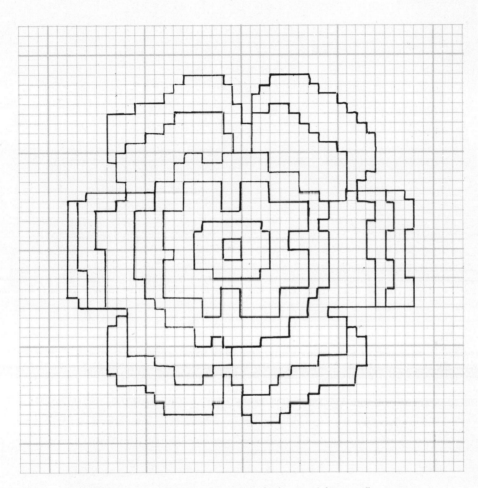

Pre-Columbian Mexican floral (Xochitl) motif from a flat stamp.
Suitable for small picture or repeat design for larger picture or
pillow.

derbird designs. *(Opposite above)* Pueblo. *(Opposite below)* Pima. Suitable for
picture, pocket, patch or small purse (with zipper across the top).

23

Black-and-white pottery design painted inside a bowl from the Mimbres Valley, New Mexico. Suitable for pillow or picture.

Black-and-white pottery design painted inside a bowl from the Mimbres Valley, New Mexico. Suitable for pillow or picture.

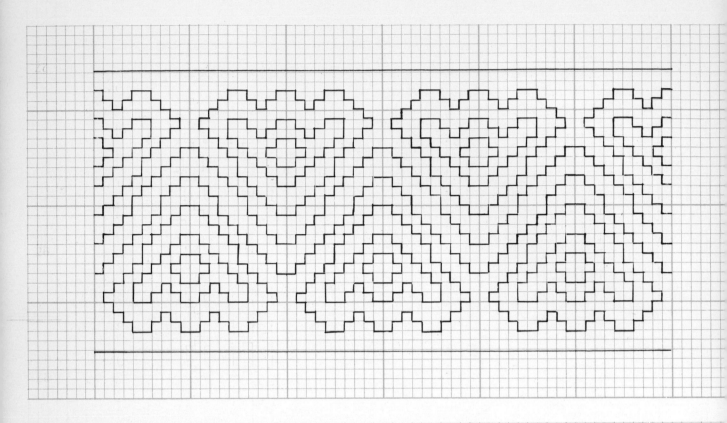

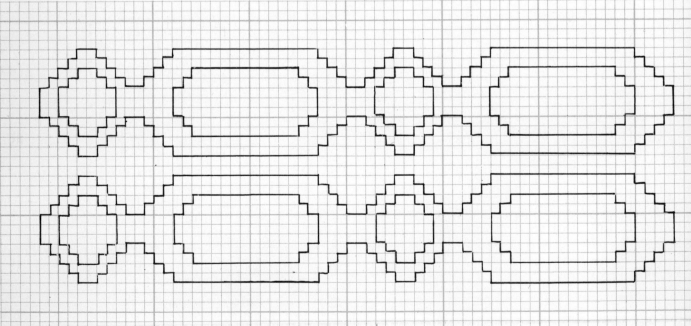

Motifs from Ojibway (Chippewa) headband designs, originally worked in feathers.
Suitable for headbands or belts or in borders.

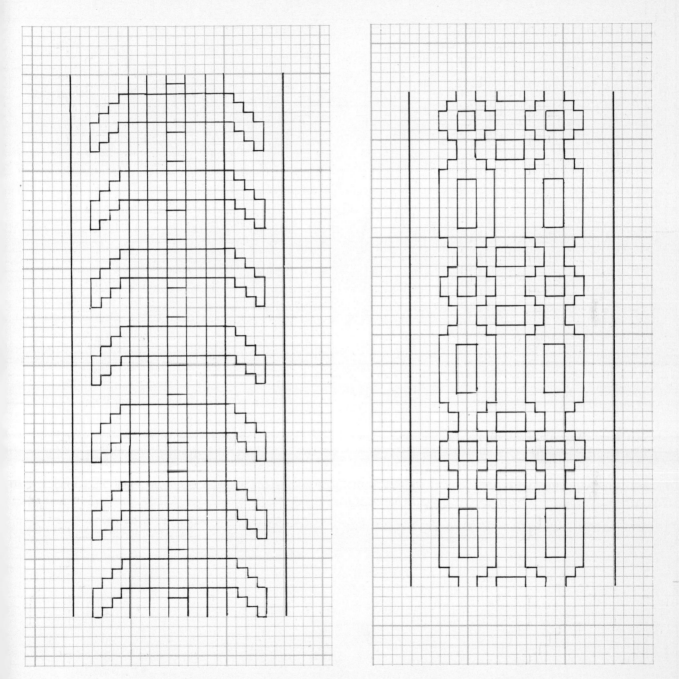

Ojibway (Chippewa) designs. Suitable for belts, headbands or in borders.

Design from an Ojibway (Chippewa) beaded pouch. Suitable for pillow or picture.

Kwakiuti (Pacific Coast) bear mask. Suitable for picture or pillow.

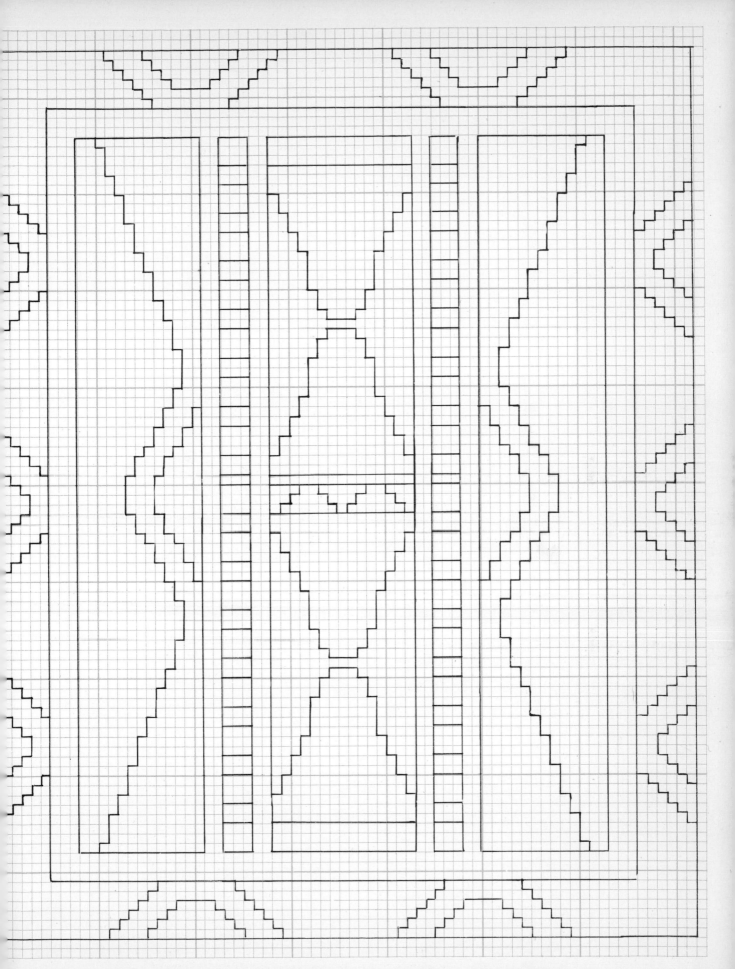

Design painted on a Sioux rawhide folding wallet. Suitable for picture or pillow.

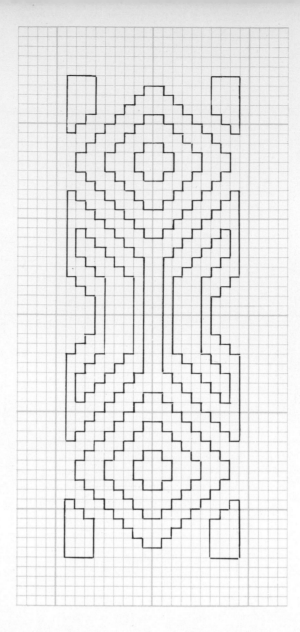

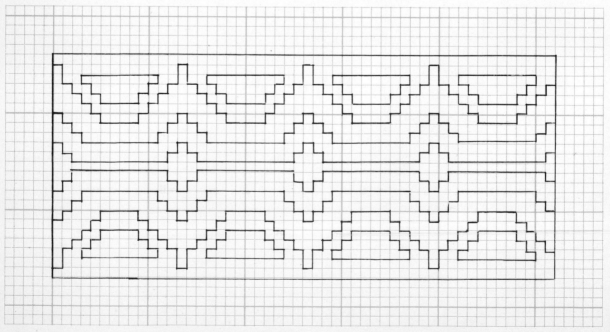

Potawatomi (Algonquin) designs. Suitable for belts, headbands, luggage straps or in borders.

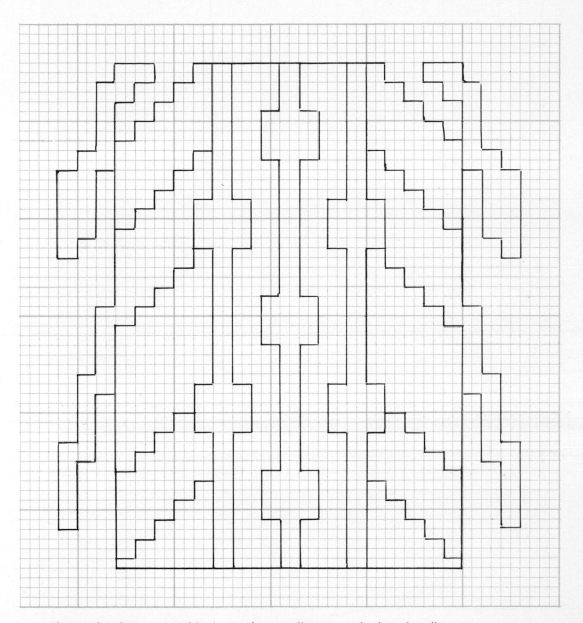

Chitimacha design. Suitable for pocket, small purse with chain handle or as a repeat pattern on a pillow or rug.

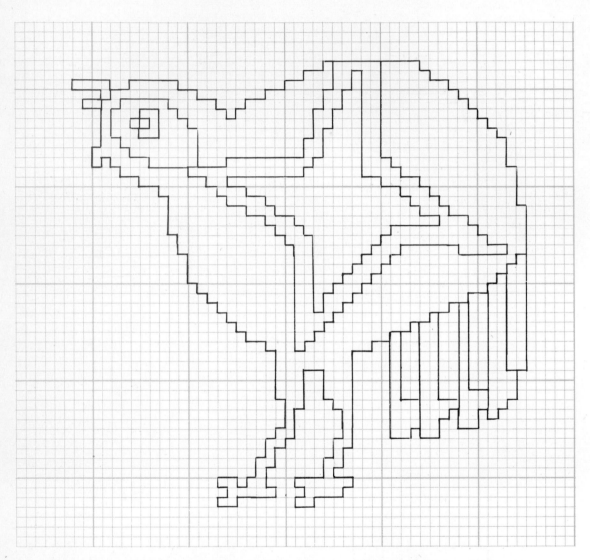

Black-and-white pottery design painted inside a bowl from the Mimbres Valley, New Mexico. Suitable for picture.

Pre-Columbian Mexican flat stamp from Teotihuacan using the rattlesnake a decorative pattern. Suitable for picture or wall hanging.

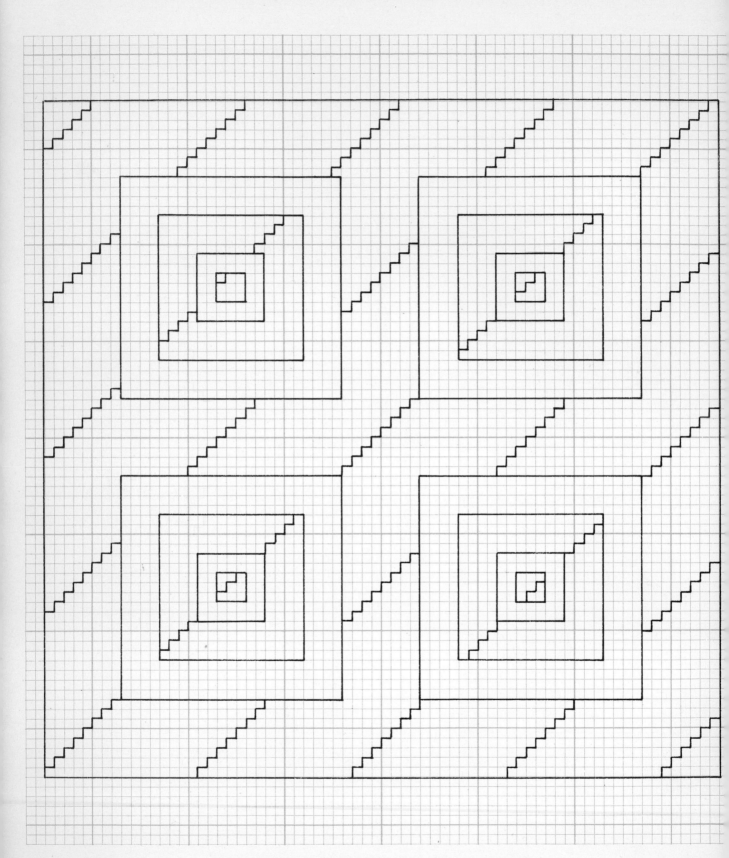

Choctaw design. Suitable for picture, pillow or wall hanging.

Design from Sauk and Fox beadwork. Suitable for pillow, picture or as a repeat for carpet design.

9834